The Foreclosure Mediation Training Guide

by Victoria Ring, CEO
and Certified Paralegal
http://www.713training.com

First printing, May 2007
Second printing, January 2009
ISBN: 0-9788782-1-3
LCCN: 2007927521

ATTENTION CORPORATIONS, UNIVERSITIES, COLLEGES, AND PROFESSIONAL ORGANIZATIONS. Quantity discounts are available on bulk purchases of this book for educational, gift purposes or as premiums for increasing magazine subscriptions or renewals. Special books or book excerpts can also be produced to fit specific needs.

For information, please contact Graphico Publishing, 1601 West Fifth Avenue, Suite 123, Columbus, Ohio 43212-2303 or http://www.graphicopublishing.com.

Graphico Publishing
a subsidiary of 713Training.Com, LLC
1601 West Fifth Avenue, Suite 123
Columbus, Ohio 43212-2303
Website: http://www.graphicopublishing.com

The Foreclosure Mediation Training Guide

by Victoria Ring, CEO
and Certified Paralegal
http://www.713training.com

Legal Disclaimer

The author, Victoria Ring is <u>NOT</u> an attorney.

The information contained in *The Foreclosure Mediation Training Guide* is for training purposes only and should not be considered legal advice.

All the material in this book is written from the perspective of Victoria Ring, an experienced bankruptcy paralegal who has never attended law school and is not authorized to practice law in any state.

The author and publisher do not warrant or guarantee any of the website references or products described herein. By following the instructions contained herein, the reader willingly assumes all risks in connection with any transactions.

The author and publisher make no representations or warranties of any kind; nor are any such representations implied with respect to the material set forth herein, and the author and publisher takes no responsibility with respect to such material   The author and publisher shall not be liable for any special, consequential, or exemplary damages resulting in whole or in part from the reader's use of, or reliance upon this material.

Table of Contents

SECTION 1

SECTION 3

SECTION 4

SECTION 1
The Basics, Set-Up and Structure of starting a Foreclosure Mediation Service

Introduction

The other day I was watching a commercial about enrolling in truck driving school. The advertiser pointed out all the wonderful benefits of being a truck driver. In only three short weeks I would be able to travel all over the country, make excellent money, and never worry about unemployment again. The commercial showed a big 18-wheeler driving down beautiful scenic highways. Mountains, lakes and streams were dominating the background and the truck driver was smiling from ear-to-ear.

For a moment, I found myself lost into the dream of being a truck driver and I was actually considering enrolling in the school for a brief moment. But thank the Lord, my mind returned to reality. I suddenly remembered all the bad points about the trucking industry.

A friend of mine been married to a truck driver for almost 40 years. I know first hand that driving an 18-wheeler is no picnic. The job is very hard on the body. Long road trips cause many physical problems and almost all truckers end up with severe back problems later in life. Also, you have to work your tail off to make money as a truck driver. You must "beat the clock" while fighting traffic problems as well as severe weather. There also are a lot of government regulations that truckers must adhere to which complicate their job. These regulations include irritants such as mandatory weigh-in stations (which adds more time to their trip) and preparing detailed, repetitive paperwork.

When you take the time to look past the "money" you will find that everything you do in life requires you to enjoy what you are doing. If not, you will face an endless stream of failures, disappointments and a depressing life filled with no meaning or purpose.

But how will you know if you like a job well enough to enjoy it, if you have never done the job? In many cases, you will have to try it out - or talk to several people (not one person) who has experience working the job you are excited about. However, you will always learn best by experiencing the job yourself. Then, if you don't like it, move on to something else until you find the type of work you enjoy doing.

In my case, after talking with my friend about the bad side of truck driving, I was convinced it was not for me. In fact, if someone offered me $100 per hour to sit inside a truck and travel 3,000 miles, I would turn them down without hesitation. I know that truck driving is not for me and never will be. It doesn't mean that I am stupid and cannot do the job. It simply means that the job does not fit my personality as well as my goals.

The same holds true with Foreclosure Mediation and YOU. This job is not for everyone; in fact, no job is. But I have tried my best to include everything I know about Foreclosure Mediation in this book so you will be able to make a more informed decision about whether to become a Foreclosure Mediator or not. Although you can make a great deal of money working as a Foreclosure Mediator, if you do not like the job or have the desire to work hard to improve your skills to perfection, you will not make any money. People with this attitude always blame the world for their inability to succeed which does nothing for productivity.

Therefore, I hope you take the time to absorb all the information in this book and not just skim through it. In fact, I urge you to read it a couple of times if you are seriously considering working as a Foreclosure Mediator. It is important for you to fully understand the type of work involved so that you can determine whether this job fits your personality or not. Then you can move forward.

Do You Need Experience to Work as a Foreclosure Mediator?

Some people do and some people don't. I remember when I trained a guy named Andy how to prepare bankruptcy petitions. He brought his laptop to my house and we spent about an hour drafting a petition. Andy had studied my training materials and already had practiced doing petitions before he came to me for training. If he had not prepared, he would have been lost.

However, in only 60 minutes, Andy was able to take the knowledge he learned from me and within 30 days he was working as a virtual assistant for five different bankruptcy attorneys. Within a year he had moved up to Foreclosure Mediation and was making even more money compared to doing bankruptcy petitions. And two years after that, he became part owner of a bank, purchased a pizza shop and even bought several properties, fixed them up and made even more money.

Andy is one of those success stories that amazes me everything I think about it. However, most people are not like Andy. Andy is just one of those types of people that does not need a college education or experience in a job to succeed. Instead, he "takes the ball and runs with it." It is second nature to him.

On the other hand, there are people who study training materials, follow all the instructions and do everything they can in order for their business to make money; but they do not succeed. I was one of those people when I started my first business in 1988. Although I failed financially my first year, I learned so many valuable lessons that the education was worth more than a million dollars.

Therefore, you should be able to understand why I am unable to tell you whether you need experience to succeed as a Foreclosure Mediator or not. However, I do think a good knowledge of bankruptcy and working with the mortgage industry are two plus's in your favor. That is why I am bringing this knowledge to the virtual bankruptcy assistants as well as the notary signing agents. People with experience in either field have the basic knowledge to work as Foreclosure Mediators and do very well.

In fact, I wish I would have known about this field back in 1988. The start-up costs are less than $10.00 (for your forms) and the fore-closure market is growing rapidly. This is the perfect time to work as a Foreclosure Mediator and the skills you learn will be priceless.

General Overview

I was first introduced to the world of Foreclosure Mediation by Andy, the guy I trained in preparaing bankruptcy petitions. This was his way of returning the favor.

Back in June 2005, Andy was our special guest at a bankruptcy teleconference. He had learned about Foreclosure Mediation from a bankruptcy attorney he was working for at the time. Andy was drafting a bankruptcy petition when he encountered a client that was going to lose her home to foreclosure. The attorney trained Andy in putting together a "Work-Out Plan" between the lender and the client so that the client could stay in her home and still file a Chapter 7. (She was unable to fund a Chapter 13 due to her low income.)

Suddenly, the whole idea of Foreclosure Mediation became fascinating to me and I began researching the topic on the internet. Also, I was attracted to the fact this is was probably another one of those "golden nuggets" where people like you can make an excellent income with low overhead costs. Plus, performing services as a Foreclosure Mediator will benefit the lives of people and this should make your work personally fulfilling.

The Fraudulent Side of the Foreclosure Mediation Field

Before we learn the right way to do Foreclosure Mediation, I want to make you aware of the fraud that is rampant within the foreclosure industry. That way, when you run into it (and you will), you will be able to recognize the fraud and understand it for what it is.

If you have lived on this planet for any length of time, you are aware that every time an honest and worthwhile idea is introduced, some greedy and deceitful people take that idea and twist it around for their own financial benefit. These greedy people have done the same thing in the Foreclosure Mediation world. These fraudulent operators set up "fake" Foreclosure Mediation services with the sole intent of stealing assets from Borrowers. Watch for these types of companies and report them to the proper authorities (if possible) for investigation when you encounter them.

However, if you take the time to research the world of foreclosure, you will find individuals and even large companies who buy assets from

Borrowers who are either in foreclosure or filing bankruptcy. After buying the assets (homes, cars, equipment, machinery, etc.) for an extremely low price, they resell it and make a huge profit. Although buying and reselling assets is not fraud, it becomes fraud when someone sets up a service designed to lure Borrowers in with lies and deception. The person that loses in this type of fraud is the Borrower who is left homeless and was taken advantage of financially. It is very sad when things like this happen to innocent people and I hope you do not get involved in this type of fraudulent business.

In summary, if you have the skills, the desire and the interest to work as a Foreclosure Mediator; be sure to set your business up so that it is a benefit to others. In doing so, you will earn an excellent income, plus you will never have to spend every waking moment worried about when you will be "caught." Since fraud is so short-lived, it only makes logical sense to run your business legitimately and with the heart to help and benefit others. There are more benefits than you can imagine when you operate your business in this manner.

What is Foreclosure Mediation?

Okay. Let's dig right in and start learning the skills you purchased this book for.

Foreclosure mediation is a process whereby a Foreclosure Mediator (like you) negotiates with the Servicing Company to work out a Work-Out Plan to repay a mortgage loan. This Work-Out Plan must be fair and impartial for both the lender and the Borrower. In most cases, Foreclosure Mediation will help to save the Borrower's credit, keep them in their home (or other real property) and save their equity.

Foreclosure Mediation can also work in reverse. If the Borrower(s) wish to surrender their property, the lender will normally agree to a cash settlement to pay for moving expenses. This is normally handled as a Deed-in-Lieu of Foreclosure and it saves the lender thousands of dollars in foreclosure fees.

However, every Foreclosure Mediation you become involved with will be unique and different. You will discover that there are a wide variety of facts that can change and alter the average Foreclosure Mediation case. Some cases you work with will be simple and easy. Others will be hard and almost impossible. Some Borrowers will be cooperative and provide you with everything you need, others will need reassurance and mental support, others will be rude and vicious and other Borrowers will never return your phone calls.

Therefore, before starting any Foreclosure Mediation you must assess the facts. These are explained in detail beginning on Page 55 of this book.

Why do People Get Behind in Mortgage Payments?

When a Borrower falls behind in their mortgage payments, it does not necessarily mean they are a deadbeat or bad person. In most instances, the opposite is true. According to a National U.S. study, people normally get behind in their mortgage payments because of:

- Illness or injury
- Job loss
- Divorce or separation
- Unexpected repairs or expenses
- Unexpected medical emergencies
- Inability to successfully prioritize debts

All of these situations are normally out of the control of the Borrower(s) and most lenders are willing to work with them to negotiate a Work-Out Plan. Remember that lenders are people too. They understand that things in life can happen; but the bottom line is: they want their money and they are willing to bend a little to get it.

Why Would a Mortgage Company Be Willing to Negotiate a Work-Out Plan?

Many people new to this field believe that lenders love foreclosing on a piece of property and there is nothing anyone can do to stop them. However, the opposite is true. It costs a lender thousands of dollars in expenses to go through the foreclosure process, Sheriff's sale and Deed transfer fees. Therefore, many lenders are willing to negotiate a Work-Out Plan to save them time and money. This is where your services as a Foreclosure Mediator come in.

Think about it. If the neighbor across the street borrowed $100 from you and was unable to pay it back all at once; would you accept $50 now and $50 next week? Of course you would. Why? Because the neighbor is sincere in trying to pay you back. Besides, just like lenders, the bottom line is: you want your money.

However, if your neighbor avoided you and never mentioned they owed you $100, how would you feel? Would you be willing to give them another $100 when they asked for it? Of course not. In fact, you would probably get angry with your neighbor and the $100 would have a detrimental effect on your relationship forever.

With the same thought in mind, place yourself in the shoes of the lender when you are negotiating a Work-Out Plan. The Borrower owes the lender money. The lender wants their money. The Borrower cannot afford to pay the lender all the money they owe them at once. Therefore, the lender is normally willing to work with the Borrower if you (as a Foreclosure Mediator) show the Borrower is sincere and will stick with their Work-Out Plan to pay the lender back their money.

But at the same time you are negotiating, you cannot have the entire Work-Out Plan benefit the lender (just because you want to present a Plan that will be approved.) You must also keep the Borrower's needs in mind and get them the best deal you can. This balancing act will take some time and experience to build, but if you keep working at it, you can become a very successful Foreclosure Mediator. Perhaps one day, you will be writing your own book or holding seminars to teach others the personal experience and success you have enjoyed.

> **HINT:** Gathering the financial information and putting together a Work-Out Plan as a Foreclosure Mediator is a very similar skill to preparing a Chapter 13 Plan in bankruptcy. So once you learn the skill and have experience as a Foreclosure Mediator, you can earn an additional income for your business if you provide virtual Chapter 13 services to bankruptcy attorneys.

How Foreclosure Mediation Works in Bankruptcy Cases

Many of you who will be working in Foreclosure Mediation will also be preparing bankruptcy petitions for attorneys as a virtual assistant. This situation provides you with a distinct advantage because you will be working with people who are having trouble paying their mortgage. Some bankruptcy attorneys are unaware of the benefits of Foreclosure Mediation and if you have this knowledge, you and the attorney can make an additional income and help the Borrower(s) at the same time.

Foreclosure Mediation can be done before, during and after a bankruptcy has been initiated. (When a bankruptcy is completed it is either "discharged" or "dismissed.") Although you can perform your duties as a Foreclosure Mediator without working under an attorney, you will find that it is easier when you do. One advantage of working under an attorney is that when you call a Servicer to negotiate a Work-Out Plan, you normally gain more leverage and recognition when you say: *"Hello. My name is John Doe. I am calling for attorney Joe Brown."*

Additionally, when a Borrower is filing bankruptcy, this will always give you more leverage during a negotiation with a Servicer. Because bankruptcy is federal law and carries a great deal of weight in discharging debts, the Servicers would rather negotiate a Work-Out Plan than lose more money if the Borrower files bankruptcy.

In a bankruptcy case, if a Borrower is filing a Chapter 7 and they are in the process of a foreclosure, they normally do not have enough money left over to pay the lender all the back-due arrearages before their 341 Meeting of Creditors (approximately 6 weeks after filing the bankruptcy petition.) Unless the arrearages are paid in full by this time, there is little chance the lender (creditor) will reaffirm on the debt and allow the Borrower(s) to keep their property. This is why some attorneys advise their clients to file a Chapter 13 so they can keep their property, stop the foreclosure and pay back the arrearages over 3-5 years.

But the problem arises when people who need to file a Chapter 13 to protect their property and pay the arrearages back over a period of time cannot qualify for a Chapter 13. In a Chapter 13 bankruptcy, the person needs to have a regular income, be able to pay their basic living expenses, and still have enough money left over to make a payment to the Bankruptcy Trustee. The Bankruptcy Trustee takes this money and distributes it to the creditors the person owes money to. If the person is unable to make this payment and/or is unemployed, they have no choice but to file a Chapter 7. This places them in danger of losing their property since they cannot pay the past due arrearages before the 341 Meeting of Creditors.

However, if the person has the ability to qualify for a Chapter 13 bankruptcy, the foreclosure issue is immediately resolved. This is due to the fact that in a Chapter 13, the debtor(s) are normally paying their arrearages (the amount of money they are behind in payments) inside the Chapter 13 Plan. A Chapter 13 bankruptcy lasts up to 5 years, which gives the people enough time to pay back all the arrearages.

But a Chapter 7 bankruptcy does not have a Plan payment and the people are rarely in the bankruptcy for more than 3 or 4 months. Therefore, the arrearages (which could be thousands of dollars if the debtors are in fore-closure) will be a major problem for the debtors to pay all at once and the debtor(s) may be forced to surrender their property.

Example of a Work-Out Plan in Bankruptcy

John Doe is $7,000 in arrears on his mortgage. He has 25 years left before the mortgage is paid off. The Foreclosure Mediator makes an offer to the Servicer to extend the mortgage loan from 25 years to 28 years and put $6,000 in arrears inside the new recalcu-lated loan and Chapter 13 Plan. Joe would then make a "good faith" lump sum payment of $1,000 and John is allowed to remain in his home. Additionally, in many circumstances,

John's monthly mortgage payment may also be reduced when the loan is recalculated.

What if the Borrower(s) Want to Surrender Their Home?

As previously mentioned, Foreclosure Mediation can also work in reverse if the Chapter 7 debtor(s) wish to surrender their home. Suppose Jack Sprat cannot afford to continue making the $1,200 monthly mortgage payments now that his wife has died. He decides to file bankruptcy and surrender his home. The Foreclosure Mediator may offer the Servicer a Work-Out Plan to save them the expense of a foreclosure by having Jack sign a Deed-in-Lieu.

Jack Sprat will turn over the deed to his property – saving the lender $7,000 or more in foreclosure fees and attorney costs. Often, the lender will even pay an amount of $2,000 or more (depending on the equity, market value, etc. of the property) so Jack will have money for moving expenses. In exchange, Jack agrees to leave the property in resalable condition by making all necessary repairs, painting and cleaning all the carpets.

Can a Borrower Do Their Own Negotiation?

Yes. The Borrower should be encouraged to contact their lender before they face a foreclosure. However, if the Borrower is unable to reach a successful negotiation within 1 to 2 weeks, this is a relatively clear indication that the lender has little interest in dealing with the Borrower directly.

Unfortunately though, if a foreclosure has already begun, the lender has probably turned the collection procedure over to a foreclosure attorney.

It is highly unlikely the Borrower will be able to speak to the foreclosure attorney, let alone negotiate with them to keep their property. In fact, corporate attorneys will normally only respond through formal channels. This is where your services as a Foreclosure Mediator will be in high demand because you will work through the formal channels for the Borrowers and handle the negotiation process to save their property.

How Can Virtual Bankruptcy Assistants Profit From This Knowledge?

Virtual bankruptcy assistants are people who work under the direction of bankruptcy attorneys as an independent contractor. The difference between an employee and a virtual bankruptcy assistant is that they work from their home office. This reduces overhead expenses for the law firm by 70% or more simply because virtual bankruptcy assistants pay their own overhead expenses and taxes. Additionally, virtual bankruptcy assistants specialize in bankruptcy and have more knowledge in drafting petitions compared to many law firm employees.

But the fact remains, a virtual bankruptcy assistant you can earn an additional income by performing Foreclosure Mediation services for the bankruptcy attorneys they work for. They can accomplish this simply because they are already drafting petitions and have the "insider knowledge" to be in touch with people who need their Foreclosure Mediation services.

How Can Notary Signing Agents Profit From This Knowledge?

Notary signing agents can also add Foreclosure Mediation to their existing business, but they will need to locate people who need their services. As a notary signing agent closing loans, you are operating on the "other side" of the foreclosure fence. Borrowers who are purchasing or refinancing their property are not facing a foreclosure at the time they close their loan. Therefore, these people do not need your services as a Foreclosure Mediator.

So, as a notary signing agent, if you want to add Foreclosure Mediation to your list of services, you will need to either: (1) Work independently for other companies who perform Foreclosure Mediation services until you build up a clientele of your own; (2) Research online and find lists of people who are facing foreclosure so you can contact them directly; or (3) Network with debt consolidation services that will refer business to you.

In other words, as a notary signing agent, you do not have the "insider knowledge" that a virtual bankruptcy assistant has who is exposed to foreclosures through the bankruptcy petitions they draft. However, you can still make this business work; and the financial rewards are better than most employers can offer you in a full-time job.

How Much Money Can You Earn as a Foreclosure Mediator?

First and foremost, I cannot answer this question for you. No one can. You are the only person that can determine how much money you will make. It all depends on your skills, knowledge, approach, the quality of your service and a variety of other factors. Because I have never met you, I cannot tell you how much money you will make.

However, I can tell you how much money other people have made as a Foreclosure Mediator. Andy (the gentleman I previously mentioned) sent me the following email:

"I earn as much as 75% of the attorney fee when I do Foreclosure Mediation. If the attorney charges the client $1,000, the attorney normally pays me $750 because I do most of the work. In my opinion, $750 for about 2 hours of my time is fantastic money."

Victoria Rivera in St. Port Joe, Florida has also added Foreclosure Mediation to her virtual bankruptcy assistant business. She told me on the telephone:

"My knowledge of the mortgage industry was a plus in helping me know how to negotiate with banks and mortgage companies. So far, 3 of the 5 bankruptcy petitions I have drafted qualified for Foreclosure Mediation.

I am sure I will never run out of business as a Foreclosure Mediator."

How to Price Foreclosure Mediation Services

Before you run out and put up a billboard offering your Foreclosure Mediation services, take a moment and do a little research. It will not cost you a dime.

On Page 172, I have provided a short list of companies that provide Foreclosure Mediation services. Study their websites and educate yourself about how they have structured their businesses as well as the fees they charge. Download some of their forms that are used to gather information from their customers and decide for yourself if Foreclosure Mediation is something you will enjoy doing. If so, you can continue your research and pursue this financially rewarding field.

But for those of you on the "outside looking in" who need an idea of the type of money you can make as a Foreclosure Mediator, we can follow the example Andy gave us. He charged the attorney 75% of the attorney fee. In other words, the attorney charges the client $1,000 and Andy received $750. But every foreclosure is different because every person has a unique set of circumstances.

So, what happens if you do not work for a bankruptcy attorney like Andy does? How much should you charge your clients if they hire you directly for Foreclosure Mediation? Here is what Sally Farleigh, a real estate agent, told me when I discussed the subject with her:

> *"My suggestion would be to base the fee for Foreclosure Mediation on the total amount of the debt that is owed as well as on the payment history of the Borrower.*

For instance, I would charge a different fee to Sue who was $3,000 in mortgage arrears than Jane who owed her lender $10,000. I also would charge a different fee to Jack if he had a bad payment history with his lender compared to Rick who had a good payment history but recently suffered a job loss through no fault of his own. I would know that Rick's lender would be easier to mediate with compared to Jack's lender. Therefore, my fee for the Foreclosure Mediation would be different for both.

If I were forced to pull a fee out of thin air, I suppose I would start at charging a fee of 10% to 25% of the amount I am negotiating.

Therefore, if I were negotiating a total debt amount of $10,000, I would charge the Borrower a Foreclosure Mediation fee of $1,000 to $2,500 depending on their credit history. The $1,000 fee would be for a Borrower with a good payment history and $2,500 would be for the person with a bad credit payment history.

But because I have not thoroughly researched the field, I would suggest that people reading this book use my guidelines as a starting point. Compare these percentages to other companies who are actively providing Foreclosure Mediation services to determine if your pricing is in line with what the market will bear. Then, make the

*required adjustments to fit your
client base."*

Different Types of "Work-Out" Plans

There are many different types of Work-Out Plans that you will be dealing with as a Foreclosure Mediator. Each one is as unique as the Borrower themselves. At one extreme is an agreement that the Borrower will skip a certain number of mortgage payments during a job layoff or closing; then repaying those skipped payments over the next 12 months. At the other extreme is the agreement by the lender to accept a Deed-in-Lieu so that the Borrower will not owe the lender any money after the foreclosure has occurred.

Work-Out Plans that are between these two extremes will vary for every Borrower you work with as a Foreclosure Mediator. Some of these Work-Out Plans may involve reducing the interest rate, extending the length of the loan or repaying the arrears at the end or over the remaining length of the loan.

Now, that I have covered the basics as well as the set-up and structure of a Foreclosure Mediation service; let's move on to Section 2. Section 2 covers the day-to-day tasks of a Foreclosure Mediator.

SECTION 2
The Day-to-Day Business
of Operating a
Foreclosure Mediation Service

How To Get Started

First, you should provide Borrower(s) with your Forms Package to fill out, sign and return to you. Your forms package should include:

- Written Authorization
  (see sample on Page 93)
- Agreement
  (see sample on Page 95)
- Borrower(s) Intake Form
  (see sample on Page 99)

You should not make copies of the samples provided in this book. Instead, you need to make your own forms for your company because you will need to personalize them with your company name and edit the information to fit your services. There are many software programs you can use to make your forms.

Some people use MS Word, others use PageMaker; however, there are a variety of other software programs you may wish to try. Below is a list of some of these websites that you can check out:

- http://www.smartdraw.com/
- http://www.smartform.com/
- http://www.cadandgraphics.com/

Also, go to any search engine and type in the search words: "easy form software" to find many more.

Your forms should be made in a hard copy format so you can make copies to provide them to your customers as well as making them available in PDF format. That way, your customer can go to your website, download the PDF forms, print them, fill them out and return to you. This saves you printing and postage expenses as well as the time you would spend processing the request.

The Written Authorization Form

Before you can pick up the phone make the first call to the Servicer, you must obtain written authorization from the Borrower that allows you to act as a negotiator on their behalf. Before using the sample on Page 93 you should ask the Borrower to call their mortgage company and find out if they have a specific form they want you to use. If not, go ahead and use the sample on Page 93 but I cannot guarantee that it will work for every lending institution in every state. After submitting the Written Authorization to the lender, if it is not an accepted an accepted form, they will let you know. Then you can make adjustments to the Written Authorization to comply to the lender's and the state's requirements for future jobs you do.

In most cases, the Work-Out Plan must be made with the company that is servicing the loan (the department that accepts payments and issues past due notices). Work-Out Plans are not made with the lender or the party who the Borrower owes money to. Often, this department is referred to as the "Servicer" and most Servicers are large corporations.

However, since most properties you will be working with are in the middle of a foreclosure (court proceeding), there will most likely be an attorney involved that is representing the lender. In this case, the attorney of the Borrower will need to initially contact the lender's attorney in order to give the Foreclosure Mediator the authority to speak with them to arrange a Work-Out Plan for the Borrower.

Departments in a Typical Servicer Shop

To help you better understand the departments within the Servicer Shop, the following is a list (along with a basic description) of the many different departments you will encounter as a Foreclosure Mediator:

Foreclosure Department

The Foreclosure Department monitors the entire foreclosure process. You would not call this department to negotiate a Work-Out Plan. Instead, you would only contact this department to obtain copies of foreclosure notices, or to check on the status of a foreclosure and to obtain an itemization of the foreclosure fees and costs. These costs are essential to you as a Foreclosure Mediator because you will need to address these costs in the Work-Out Plan. Sometimes, you may be able to get all the foreclosure costs eliminated (if there is a benefit to the Servicer) or a reduction in the fees. But you will never know how much these costs are until you contact the Foreclosure Department.

Escrow Department

The Escrow Department handles all the money that is in held in escrow for the Borrower. This money is then used to pay for hazard insurance, property taxes, mortgage insurance and other assessments. Do not assume that every loan has an escrow attached to it. Some Borrowers elect to pay their own property taxes, insurance and other fees directly; so make sure you ask the Borrower before contacting the Escrow Department. You do not want to waste their time and yours. However, you will find that the majority of Borrowers pay an additional amount every month (along with their mortgage payment.) This amount is collected by the Escrow Department and when taxes, insurance and other fees related to the property are due, the Escrow Department pays them out of the Borrower's Escrow account. Any questions about the amount owed for escrow so you can include any negative escrow balance in the Work-Out Plan should be addressed to this department.

Collections Department

The Collections Department aggressively attempts to collect past due payments from Borrowers who fall behind in their mortgage payments. This department also has the authority to impose a variety of penalties against Borrowers in order to collect this past due money. When a Foreclosure Mediator calls the Servicer, he or she will often be routed to this Department. However, this department is very limited in their authority to negotiate a Work-Out Plan. It is much easier to contact the Loss Mitigation Department (see below).

Loss Mitigation Department

The Loss Mitigation Department has the most authority to discuss and negotiate Work-Out Plans. It is usually best to call this department directly rather than go through the main switchboard. But if you do not have the direct telephone number, the main switchboard will try to route you to the Collections Department. To avoid this problem, always begin the conversation by establishing your authority to speak on behalf of the Borrower and then ask to be transferred to the Loss Mitigation Department. However, if the Borrower has filed bankruptcy or the property has already been through the foreclosure process, refer to the next two department descriptions that follow.

Bankruptcy Department

The Bankruptcy Department handles all bankruptcy cases that are filed by Borrowers. In most cases, you will already know whether the Borrower has filed bankruptcy or not because you are working under the direction of a bankruptcy attorney.

Real Estate Owned Department

The Real Estate Owned Department will obtain the ownership of the property once the property has completed the foreclosure process. If the foreclosure process has already occurred, you will need to contact this department in order to:

- Negotiate more time for the Borrower to stay in their home;

- Discuss eviction proceedings and other related issues.

Additional Tips for Foreclosure Mediators Working With Servicers

Tip Number 1

Before starting any conversation with the Servicer, make sure you provide them with the Borrower's Written Authorization (see Page 93).

Normally you will fax or email this to a particular employee; so make sure you ALWAYS get the first and last name of the Servicer's employee when you call.

Helpful Hint: I set up a low-cost online fax account with MaxEmail at

http://www.maxemail.com

I then fax documents to my MaxEmail account and they are sent to me in PDF format. The PDF version can then be used to email as an attachment to Servicer's. Or, some Servicer's may still prefer the old fashioned method (so they have a hard copy) and ask you to fax the document to them. In this case you can fax the PDF document through MaxEmail also and it will print as a paper copy on their fax machine.

Tip Number 2

The Escrow Department will normally not know whether a Work-Out Plan was made with the Loss Mitigation Department or not. Therefore, the Escrow Department may continue billing payments for amounts you may already have included in the Work-Out Plan. Therefore, when a Work-Out Plan is approved with the Loss Mitigation Department, make sure you notify the Escrow Department also. Otherwise, this could result in a double billing for the Borrower which you do not want to happen.

Tip Number 3

From your first contact, you should always build a good working relationship with the Servicers. More than likely, you will be working with the same Servicer again and again because they normally represent several lenders. However, do not be so "soft" that you forget your goal of helping the Borrower. It is often a tricky balance to be fair to both sides while getting the most benefit for the Borrower.

However, if you work with a Servicer who is helpful, make sure you ask the Borrower to send a Thank You note to either the employee or their supervisor. Often you will need to purchase the Thank You note for the Borrower, sign your name and have the Borrower sign theirs. Then, you will also probably be responsible for mailing it. Rarely do Borrowers follow up on sending a Thank You note (no matter how many times you remind them) because it is not as important to them as it will be to you. Although it may seem very small and unimportant, a simple Thank You note will greatly aide you in establishing good business relations with the Servicer in the future.

On the other hand, if an employee is not helpful, do not argue with the employee or allow yourself to be driven to a temper tantrum. Instead, ask to speak to a supervisor in a professional business manner. If the employee refuses to transfer you, hang up and call back the main switchboard; then ask to speak to a supervisor of that department. Make sure you insist you speak with a supervisor - not an employee.

Tip Number 4

Make it a habit to always get first and last names of people you talk with. In fact, this information should be obtained before the conversation begins. For example: Normally company employees will answer your call by saying: *"This is Jane Doe, may I help you?"* If the employee does not provide their name, you should say: *"Hello, this is Peter Piper, may I ask who I am speaking with?"* Then, make sure you write this information down immediately.

Tip Number 5

Keep extremely detailed notes of every piece of information you obtain while negotiating for the Borrower. After every conversation with the Servicer, you should immediately write out a summary of the conversation into a list of notes. Always be sure to record the date and time of every conversation, who you spoke with, what was discussed, the outcome (if any), as well as any follow-up tasks you need to perform. You will find you will refer to these notes often and they will keep you very well organized and on top of everything.

Tip Number 6

If the Work-Out Plan you submit to the Servicer is rejected, don't give up. First you need to find out the reason for the rejection to make sure there are no misunderstandings as to the facts in your Work-Out Plan. Perhaps the Servicer wants more details before they can consider the Plan, which is why they rejected it at this time. If more facts are needed, you can gather the documentation and resubmit the Work-Out Plan for a second review.

Tip Number 7

Always make sure the mathematical calculations in your Work-Out Plan are current and correct. Check them several times to make sure. Nothing is more embarrassing for you as a Foreclosure Mediator to propose a Work-Out Plan with wrong accounting.

How to Put Together a Work-Out Plan

Get The Facts and Assess the Situation

In order to begin putting together a Work-Out Plan you need to first understand the objectives and needs of the Borrower. For example: Is the Borrower disputing the amount they owe the lender? Does the Borrower have the ability to pay their arrearages over a period of time (normally 12-18 months)? Does the Borrower want to sell their property, pay off the lender in full and profit from the difference? What is the future income expected by the Borrower? How much money does the Borrower pay their other creditors (such as car payment, credit cards, etc.)? In other words, you will need to interview the Borrower and assess their needs so you will know exactly how to initially approach the Servicer.

Next, obtain copies of any and all documents relating to pending foreclosure sales or any immediate court actions. Or, ask the Borrower to provide you with the case number and the name of the court the document was filed in. Look up this information on PACER at:

http://pacer.psc.uscourts.gov/

and print out the documents for the Borrower's file so you can refer to them as needed.

Additionally, ask the Borrower to notify you if they receive any additional court notices in the mail the day they arrive. They should fax or email these to you (in PDF format) so you can keep them in the file as well. But don't just file these notices without reading them over. Make sure you know what the documents are and if they require your attention before placing them inside the file. People who do not acquire this habit miss crucial dates which can causes great harm to the Borrower(s).

You will find that some court notices will be extremely important to the Borrower, while other court notices will be directed to the attorney and have no effect on the Work-Out Plan. If you are unsure what a particular court notice is, type the title of the notice into Google's search engine and do some research. This is the best way to educate yourself without spending money on seminars and books. You always want to strive to improve your skills and look for ways that allow you to grow and prosper your business.

Finally, for subprime and second mortgages, you may need to have the attorney you are working for examine the original loan documents for possible law violations. They should also be checked by the attorney to determine if the amount the lender is seeking includes excessive charges or fails to account for consumer payments.

Basic Loan Information

The Work-Out Plan needs to have the basic loan information on Page 1 for ease of identification. This information will include the full property address, full names of Borrowers, the terms of the loan, the total amount in arrears, what amount is needed to reinstate the loan as current and the total amount that is left

remaining owed on the loan. The basic information also needs to include any late fees or
foreclosure costs (if applicable.)

Also you need to provide the Servicer
with a current market value and condition of the
property. This is obtained through an appraisal
or a broker's price opinion (BPO.) Appraisals
are normally acceptable as current market
value for one year after the appraisal. Many
times Borrowers will tell you they have an appraisal, but you need to find out how old it is.
You will often find out the appraisal is several
years old which does not reflect a current market value of the Borrower's property and is
unacceptable in a Work-Out Plan to present to a
lender.

Prepare a Current Budget

Next, prepare a current budget that will
show exactly how the Borrower intends to pay

their mortgage payment as well as any arrearages they owe. You can use the information from Schedule I and J of the bankruptcy petition for the accepted categories and verbiage to construct a current budget. If you do not have a copy of the Federal Bankruptcy forms for Schedule I and J you can get them in PDF format at:

Schedule I
http://www.uscourts.gov/rules/
BK_Forms_06_Official/Form_6I_1006.pdf

Schedule J
http://www.uscourts.gov/rules/
BK_Forms_06_Official/Form_6J_1006.pdf

The current budget should also tell the lender how the Borrower plans to increase or decrease expenses in order to fully pay the amount they owe. Keep in mind that the Borrower missed several payments. The lender wants to be assured this will not happen again and the Borrower has the financial ability to repay the loan without any future problems.

Prepare a Hardship Letter

The Work-Out Plan typically includes a hardship letter. The following is an example:

Paragraph 1

The first paragraph of the Hardship Letter will provide all the basic identifying information about the property. This information includes the name, address and account number of the Borrower as well as a summary of the type of Work-Out Plan you are proposing.

Paragraph 2

The second paragraph of the Hardship Letter should describe (in detail) the reason for the hardship, its cause and changes that will occur in order to improve this hardship. Do not include personal feelings or statements about how kind and wonderful the Borrowers are. Instead, your statements need to be specific and factual. Here is an example :

> *Joe Borrower underwent a heart transplant at Wellness Hospital on May 30, 2006 which reduced his income from $4,500 per month to $1,200 per month. Joe expects to return to work with his current employer on April 27, 2007 and will have the ability to fund a successful Work-Out Plan.*

Paragraph 3

The third paragraph of the Hardship Letter provides a summary (not detail) of the income and expenses of the Borrower's. This paragraph also includes details about expected changes and the date these changes are going to occur. Also, if the Work-Out Plan includes the

Borrower making a lump sum payment (perhaps after the sale of the property), this information needs to be stated in this paragraph also. Lenders are open to lump-sum payments and will more than likely give your Work-Out Plan a higher ranking priority for review and approval if they know this information up front.

Paragraph 4

The fourth paragraph of the Hardship Letter should describe the proposed Work-Out Plan in more detail from the previous paragraph. The information also should include the following factual information:

- The starting date the Work-Out Plan is proposed to be in effect;

- The reason why the Work-Out Plan will work;

- A statement explaining why the Borrower is committed to sticking to the Work-Out Plan. Below is an example:

Borrower has demonstrated 11 years of payments that have been made on time and without interruption. Be assured that the Borrower's current financial condition is only temporary and Borrower will resume his good credit standing within 18 months of the approval of this Work-Out Plan.

Paragraph 5

The fifth or final paragraph of the Hardship Letter provides the complete contact information for the Borrower and the Borrower's attorney (if applicable). If you are directly working for the Borrower and not under the direction of an attorney, your contact information should be provided as well as your role in this case (Foreclosure Mediator) clearly identified.

Now, attach the following items to the hardship letter:

- ◆ The detailed Work-Out Plan;
- ◆ A financial statement listing the income, expenses, assets and liabilities of the Borrower.

After submitting your documents, the lender may also request the following items before making a decision:

- ◆ Recent tax returns;
- ◆ Current paycheck stubs;
- ◆ Bank account statements;
- ◆ Recent appraisal of property;
- ◆ Proof of the change in the Borrower's future income or other documentation to verify the future income or other

facts that you provided in the hardship letter or the Work-Out Plan.

Fannie Mae Work-Out Options

As a Foreclosure Mediator, you will eventually become familiar with Fannie Mae. Fannie Mae (The Federal National Mortgage Association) is the largest purchaser of mortgages on the secondary market and they set the industry standard for Work-Out options. These standards are provided free online in their Servicing Guide at:

http://www.efanniemae.com/sf/guides/ssg

Who Qualifies for Fannie Mae Work-Out Options?

Fannie Mae Work-Out options are available to Borrowers who are experiencing financial hardship, generally as a result of a substantial, involuntary reduction in income or unavoidable increase in expenses, such as a job layoff, a pay reduction, death, disability or illness in the family, or a natural disaster.

In other words, a Fannie Mae Work-Out Plan will not work for Borrowers who simply mismanaged their money or forgot to pay their house payment. For these problems, Borrowers may be encouraged to either consult with a debt counseling service or a licensed bankruptcy attorney.

This is one reason why it is beneficial for you to have several bankruptcy attorneys "in your corner" just in case the Borrower needs legal advice. Remember, as a non-attorney you cannot provide legal advice. So be very careful. Cases have been filed against non-attorneys for unauthorized practice of law and I am sure you do not want to be one of them.

Temporary Relief Measures

If the Borrower can pay all their arrears and bring their loan current; or if the Borrower wishes to sell the property in order to avoid foreclosure, Fannie Mae allows its Servicers to offer at least three forms of temporary relief. These forms of relief are:

Temporary Indulgence

A temporary indulgence is a 30-day grace period to allow the Borrower enough time to repay all past-due installments at one time. This would apply to Borrowers who are selling the property in order to make a large lump-sum payment to the lender.

Example: A 70-year old Borrower invested their entire savings as well as their retirement and 401K into purchasing stock.

The Borrower lost everything except his home valued at $245,000 and was left with a monthly income of only $402 from social security. Because the Borrower could not qualify for a loan and did not have the income to make the mortgage payment, he sold his home for $245,000, paid the lender $100,000 and was able to put $145,000 in his pocket. The other alternative was to walk away and give the property back to the bank. However, if the Borrower had done this, he would have lost the $145,000 profit, plus he would have been penniless.

Repayment Plan

In a repayment plan, the Borrower must make the current mortgage payment as well as all the past-due monies within a period of time. To determine if this would be a feasible plan, you must look at all the Borrower's income. You would start by deducting all their necessary monthly expenses including the mortgage payment. If you find there is only a few dollars left over, you would be unable to prove to the lender that the Borrower will be able to pay the past-due amount. However, if the Borrower gets a second job or has a home business, this additional income may be enough to convince the lender that the Borrower can afford to enter into the Repayment Plan.

Special Forbearance

In a Special Forbearance, the Borrower will be allowed to either make reduced mortgage payments or no mortgage payments for a specific period of time. This would apply to Borrowers who are employed in jobs where they only receive income during some months and are layed off work the other months.

However, after the period allowed to the Borrower of having reduced payments or no payments at all, they must be able to resume the regular mortgage payments plus an additional amount. The additional amount that is paid each month on top of the regular mortgage payment is applied to the arrearages. There is a time limit. The arrearages must be paid in full within 18 months unless special approval is granted.

Waiver of Late Fees

Because late charges normally complicate a situation where the Borrower is unable to make mortgage payments, Fannie Mae allows its Servicers the authority to use discretion in certain hardship cases. The Servicer has the ability to waive or defer late charges.

Work-Out Plans for Serious Hardship Cases

There are four Work-Out options offered by Fannie Mae that pertain to serious hardship cases. Fannie Mae and the insurance company must approve these options. These options are:

Loan Modification

A Loan Modification will permanently change the terms of the mortgage note. Some types of modifications may include:

- Reducing the interest rate
- Changing an adjustable mortgage to a fixed rate
- Extending the length of the loan
- Capitalizing delinquent payments

A Loan Modification will normally involve additional fees that are paid to the Servicer for their overhead expenses. Sometimes, Fannie Mae will help pay a portion of these fees.

Mortgage Assumption

In a Mortgage Assumption another person transfers the loan into their name and is responsible for making the mortgage payment. The person must qualify for the loan and the property cannot be worth less than the amount owed on it. In other words, if the amount left owed on the mortgage is $150,000, and the market value of the property is only $50,000; a Mortgage Assumption will not be approved. Servicer's charge between $400 and $900 for handling the Mortgage Assumption if the Mortgage Note and local laws allow.

Pre-Foreclosure Sale

In a Pre-Foreclosure Sale, Fannie Mae will allow the Borrower to sell the property and agree to accept a lower amount than the total amount owed as full payment. This situation may occur when a Borrower decides to take a 125% loan-to-value on their property. Or, the situation may occur (where the property is worth less than the amount owed) if the property values have dropped since the Borrower purchased the property.

Example: Joe Duncan owes $300,000 to Fannie Mae but the most he can sell the property for is $225,000. If approved, Fannie Mae will accept a lump-sum payment of $225,000 and take the $75,000 loss.

However, Fannie Mae will not approve a Pre-Foreclosure sale until after all other possible alternatives have been considered. This is a logical approach since Fannie Mae cannot afford to suffer large financial losses like they would in a Pre-Foreclosure sale.

Deed-in-Lieu of Foreclosure

A Deed-in-lieu of foreclosure should only be used as a last resort where a Pre-Closure sale is not working. In this type of Work-Out the Borrower will give clear title to Fannie Mae in exchange for discharging their debt. Although the Borrower ends up with nothing, this option is normally more favorable than going through a foreclosure and ruining the credit of the Borrower for a longer period of time compared to a Deed-in-Lieu.

Also, as a Foreclosure Mediator, you may be able to obtain the approval of getting a few $100 or a few $1,000 for the Borrower in order to help them pay moving expenses to vacate the property. The reason the Servicer will often approve this is because the foreclosure process is very expensive ($6,000 or even more) and by giving up the property, the Borrower is saving the lender these additional costs.

Contact Information for Fannie Mae

If you are working with a Servicer for Fannie Mae and they are not being cooperative in working out a plan of repayment with the Borrower, you need to contact Fannie Mae.

Below is their contact phone numbers:

Midwest Region 312-368-6200

States: IL, IN, IA, MI, MN, NE, ND, OH, SC and WI

Northeast Region 215-575-1400

States: CT, DE, ME, MA, NH, NJ, NY, PA, PR, RI, VT and VI

Southeast Region 404-398-6000

States: AL, DC, FL, GA, KY, MD, MS, NC, SC, TN, VA and WV

Southwest Region 972-773-4663

States: AZ, AR, CO, KS, LA, MO, NM, OK, TX and UT

West Region 626-396-5100

States: AK, CA, GU, HW, ID, MT, NV, OR, WA and WY

Freddie Mac Work-Out Options

The Federal Home Loan Mortgage Corporation (Freddie Mac) is the second largest purchaser of mortgages on the secondary market. Many of Freddie Mac's Work-Out options are the same as Fannie Mae. Therefore, instead of repeating myself, I will only address the different options that Freddie Mac provides.
As a reference, their Seller Servicing Guide is available online at:

http://www.allregs.com/tpl/Main.aspx

One difference between Freddie Mac and Fannie Mae is that when Fannie Mae provides a "temporary indulgence," Freddie Mac provides the Borrower with a full reinstatement option at any time. They also allow for partial reinstatement of the loan whereby the Borrower pays less than the total amount of the arrearages; at which time the Borrower would enter into a payment plan for the balance.

Another difference between Freddie Mac and Fannie Mae is that Fannie May provides a Forbearance Plan that normally requires the full payment within 18 months. The maximum for Freddie Mac is 15 months.

Both Freddie Mac and Fannie Mae have similar Work-Out options for Loan Modifications, Assumptions and Pre-Foreclosure Sales (Freddie Mac calls it "Short Payoff") as well as Deed-in-Lieu that were previously covered.

Contact Information for Freddie Mac

If you are working with a Servicer for Freddie Mac and they are not being cooperative in working out a plan of repayment with the Borrower, you need to contact Freddie Mac at **1-800-FREDDIE**. Be sure to ask to speak with a customer service representative or the name and telephone number of an employee in the

Loss Mitigation Department who can review a Work-Out Plan.

FHA-Insured Loan Work-Out Plans

The Federal Housing Administration (FHA) is a part of the Department of Housing and Urban Development (HUD). They insure loans that eligible Borrowers (often lower income and first time home buyers) enter into with private mortgage lenders. These loans are then packaged into pools, and guaranteed by the Government National Mortgage Association (Ginnie Mae). A Servicer will handle the loan collection and the Servicer will follow HUD guidelines as to collection and Work-Put Plans. All FHA insured handbooks, guides and mortgagee letters are available at:

http://www.hud.gov/offices/adm/hudclips/index.cfm

Owners of FHA-insured loans must consider six loss mitigation options before proceeding to foreclosure. However, keep in mind that a foreclosure can proceed even while agreement on any of these six Work-Out Plans is being negotiated.

Special Forbearance

Special Forbearance (which normally happens when the Borrower is at least three months behind in payments) allows the Borrower to stop making payments for a period of time, or get a reduction in payments so the Borrower can recover from the cause of the default. The Work-Out Plan must include an explanation as to how the Borrower will eventually be able to catch up all the back payments.

Streamline Refinance

A Streamline Refinance allows a Borrower who is no more than two months in arrears to replace the existing FHA insured loan with a new loan. The new loan will have different terms, such as a different interest rate, a longer term to pay back the loan, or a fixed rate instead of an adjustable rate, or vice versa. The Borrower must pay closing costs or an equivalent interest charge for this service so try to avoid this option if others are available.

Loan Modification

A Loan Modification permanently changes the loan terms to make it more affordable. The interest rate can go down, the term can be extended, and amounts in arrears can be capitalized. Any adjustable rate must be converted to a fixed rate. Also, legal fees may be paid.

Partial Claim

A Partial Claim involves HUD granting a junior mortgage loan to the Borrower in the amount of any arrears (not including late fees or foreclosure costs), which can be repaid at any time. The Borrower has to be from 4 to 12 months delinquent and have the long term financial ability to repay the mortgage loan. Also, other forms of loss mitigation previously described must not be appropriate for this case.

Pre-Foreclosure Sale

A Pre-Foreclosure Sale is a market sale of the property with an agreement that the proceeds will satisfy the mortgage debt, even if the proceeds are less than the amount due. An attempt at such a sale can delay a foreclosure sale for up to 6 months. To qualify, the property must be appraised for at least 63% of the amount owed and the minimum sale proceeds going to HUD must be 82% of the appraisal. HUD must also approve this option before it is implemented.

Deed-in-Lieu of Foreclosure

A Deed-in-Lieu of foreclosure is an agreement that transfers the deed to the property to HUD in exchange for a cancelling the loan. The Borrower will be debt free from the mortgage company but the Borrower does not receive any profit from the sale.

To encourage Servicers to consider these loss mitigation alternatives, HUD offers financial incentives from $100 to $1,000 directly to the Servicer, depending on the type of Work-Out Plan. If the Servicer is not cooperative, you can ask for help from HUD's Oklahoma City Office: 1-888-297-8685.

Work-Out Plans with Subprime Lenders and Servicers

An attorney should carefully examine subprime loans for law violations and unfair or deceptive practices. If these exist, the attorney may wish to take the case to bring a court action or use these claims as leverage in negotiating a Work-Out Plan.

If you are working independently as a Foreclosure Mediator and not under the direction of an attorney, you should contact an attorney in your area and hire them to review the legal documents for you if you are working with a subprime Servicer. Hiring an attorney on an hourly basis is not as expensive as hiring an attorney to do the entire job for you. Of course, the attorney fee should be paid by the Borrower or incorporated into your Foreclosure Mediation fee.

If, however, the attorney does uncover law violations or possible unfair or deceptive practices, you will need to contact the Borrower immediately. As a non-attorney you would

violate unauthorized practice of law if you refer the Borrower to the attorney who reviewed the documents. Instead, you can either give the attorney the Borrower's contact information, or provide the Borrower with at least two (2) names of attorneys to help them. You should never "share fees" with an attorney or accept a "referral fee" for giving them the case.
Again, this is a violation of unauthorized practice of law.

Unlike Freddie Mac or Fannie Mae, subprime lenders and Servicers rarely have established Work-Out criteria. However, if the loan is securitized, the Work-Out options may be provided in the Pooling and Servicing agreement.

Note: Securitized loans are commercial real estate loans that are pooled with other similar loans and sold as securities. They are sometimes referred to as "commercial mort-gage-backed securities."

Subprime loans may be more subject to public relations considerations if a class action or government investigation is pending. In this type of situation, consider working "down" instead of "up" at the lender or Servicer. Instead, start with someone in government relations or the General Counsel's office. The lack of strict standards can mean that there is more flexibility, allowing the Foreclosure Mediation to come up with an imaginative Work-Out Plan.

One More Alternative

Before publishing this book I was contacted by Lloyd Torres, an experienced Foreclosure Mediator in New York. He sent me the following email regarding foreclosure options:

In some states (such as New Jersey and Vermont) the foreclosure can be pushed back simply by going to the Sheriff's office. The Borrower will pay a small fee (approx $25) to push the foreclosure back 1 week.

This process is designed to help people that are facing foreclosure, however, the Borrower is only permitted to use this service a maximum of two (2) postponements which buys them a total of 2 extra weeks. Normally, this provides the Borrower with more time to sell their property or file bankruptcy.

I have also heard from investors here in New York City that if you call the foreclosing attorney's and ask for an additional week to process a bankruptcy, in most cases it is granted. If not, you

*need to contact the Loss Mitigation officer
handling the case for your Borrower(s).*

2008 Housing Market Update

As you are aware, the bottom dropped
out of the housing market in 2008 and the
government had to step in with a Bail-Out Plan.
Instead of property accumulating equity, homes
dropped in value. I personally lost $90,000 in
equity during the housing market crash, which
is why I decided to stay in my home and not
sell it. Other people who had to move during
this time rented their home instead of selling;
and the real estate market took a nose dive.

However, as a Foreclosure Mediator, this is
the best time for you to negotiate with Lenders.
Example: A home is valued at $100,000. Jerry
and Elizabeth owe the Lender $140,000. If the
Lender forecloses on their property they can only

sell it for $100,000 (if they are lucky.) However, because of the bad housing market the Lender will have little chance of selling it at all.

This situation affords you, the Foreclosure Mediator, the opportunity to negotiate the payback on the loan to $100,000. This is called a "cram down" in the bankruptcy world. This can save the Borrower(s) $1,000s of dollars, and even help to lower their interest rate as well as their monthly payment.

Let's Move to the Forms

The next section contains templates of the various forms you will need in your Foreclosure Mediation service. Be sure to read the information provided for each form so you can utilize them to their full potential.

SECTION 3
Form Templates for Foreclosure Mediators

SAMPLE WRITTEN AUTHORIZATION
FROM BORROWER ALLOWING YOU TO NEGOTIATE
A WORK-OUT PLAN ON THEIR BEHALF

<u>Notice</u>: This is NOT a legal document. It is a sample written authorization that the majority of Servicers will accept so that you can negotiate on behalf of the Borrower. This letter is submitted by the Borrower on their letterhead. In most cases, you will provide this letter to the Borrower for them to sign. But since the letter needs to be coming from the Borrower because they are giving you permission to act on their behalf, the name, address, telephone number, etc. of the Borrower needs to be at the top of the letterhead - not your company.

JOHN and MARY DOE
123 Main Street
Cheyenne Wells CO 80810
(111) 555-1111

Date: _____ Loan No.: _____

Borrower: _____

Co-Borrower: _____

Mailing Address: _____

City: _____ State: ____ Zip: _____

Property Information

Address: _____

City: _____ State: ____ Zip: _____

To Whom It May Concern:

This letter is to serve as my written authorization that I, the mortgagor(s) on the above-referenced property, do hereby grant to **Name of Mortgage Company** permission to discuss all current and

---

- continued on Page 94

- continued from Page 93

future matters related to my mortgage with individuals as I may direct. The individual I have indicated below is authorized to discuss my personal financial matters in relation to the repayment of my mortgage with **Name of Mortgage Company.**

Name of Foreclosure Mediator
Relationship _____
Phone Number _____

Mortgagor(s) authorizing signature:

Borrower Signature
Date _____

Co-Borrower Signature
Date _____

AGREEMENT BETWEEN YOU AND THE BORROWER TO RETAIN YOUR SERVICES AS A FORECLOSURE MEDIATOR

<u>Notice</u>: This is NOT a legal document. It is a sample Agreement you can use as a template to make your own. Your Agreement should be signed by the Borrower before you do any work and it should outline the fees the Borrower will expect to pay so there is no surprise at the end of the job.

MY FORECLOSURE COMPANY
3333 Broad Boulevard, Suite 77
Lockbourne OH 43147
(740) 222-3333
http://www.myforeclosurecompany.com

Client(s) Name: _____
Mailing Address: _____
City: _____ State: _____ Zip: _____
Phone Number (Home): _____
Phone Number (Work): _____
Phone Number (Cell): _____
Email Address: _____
Servicer: _____
Mortgage Co: _____
Loan Number: _____

By signing this Agreement I (we) elect to hire **Mary Doe,** a Foreclosure Mediator, to assist me (us) in pursuing a Work-Out Plan on my (our) behalf for the mortgage loan referenced above. Upon receipt of a $_____ payment to cover the cost of the Work-Out Plan, **Mary Doe** agrees to provide the following:

    • All written correspondence to Servicers and lenders by Foreclosure Mediator will be on Foreclosure Mediator's company letterhead.

- continued on Page 96

- continued from Page 95

◆ Borrower(s) will receive a copy of all email, letters, faxes and other correspondence sent to Servicer, or received from the Servicer by the Foreclosure Mediator.

◆ Foreclosure Mediator will place the necessary calls to lender (or Servicer) to determine the exact status of Borrower's case.

◆ Foreclosure Mediator will be responsible for mediating a Work-Out Plan between Borrower(s) and lender.

◆ When applicable, Foreclosure Mediator will contact specific government agencies (i.e., Fannie Mae, Freddie Mac) for Work-Out consideration.

◆ Upon payment of fee, Foreclosure Mediator will initiate immediate communication with lender or Servicer to explore rehabilitation scenarios that have the best chance of being accepted.

◆ Foreclosure Mediator will isolate and make contact with employees of the lender who are authorized to determine Work-Out Plan eligibility.

◆ Foreclosure Mediator will prepare a professional Work-Out Plan that will be submitted to Lender (or Servicer) on the Borrower(s) behalf.

◆ Foreclosure Mediator will explore situations with the Borrower(s) that are appropriate Work-Out Plans based on in-depth analysis of Borrower(s) current financial status and future projections and forecasts.

- continued on Page 97

- continued from Page 96

◆   Borrower(s) will be provided with information regarding options to save their property.

◆   Borrower(s) have the right to cancel this Agreement without penalty or obligation within three (3) business days from the date of the signing of this Agreement and full payment of Service Fee.

Refund of Service Fees

If Borrower(s) cancel within three (3) days of the signing of this Agreement and full payment of Service Fee, Borrower(s) will be entitled to a seventy-five percent (75%) refund. If Borrower(s) cancel four (4) or more days after the signing of this Agreement and full payment of Service Fee, no refund is provided.

However, if the Foreclosure Mediator is unable or unwilling to provide you with immediate Work-Out Plan negotiation and services, a full 100% refund will be made to the Borrower(s).

Legal Disclosure

By signing below, Borrower(s) are fully aware that Foreclosure Mediator is not an attorney, in unable to practice law in any state and cannot provide legal advice. If you require the advice of an attorney, please schedule an appointment with a licensed bankruptcy attorney in your state.

I (we) understand that the services provided by **Mary Doe** (Foreclosure Mediator) is by NO means a guaran-

- continued on Page 98

- *continued from Page 97*

tee that the Lender will accept the Work-Out Plan being proposed. As such, Foreclosure Mediator accepts no liability for actions taken by the Lender, Servicer, Bank or other party.

_____

Borrower(s) Signature

_____

Printed Name
Date: _____

_____

Co-Borrower(s) Signature

_____

Printed Name
Date: _____

FORECLOSURE MEDIATOR AGREEMENT

I, **Mary Doe,** Foreclosure Mediator agree to provide the services outlined in this Agreement and provide Borrower(s) with experienced and professional services.

_____

Foreclosure Mediator
Date: _____

BORROWER(S) INTAKE FORM

Notice: This is NOT a legal document. It is a sample set of Intake Forms that you may wish to use in order to gather background information about the Borrower(s). With this information, you will be able to determine if a Work-Out Plan is possible and if you should accept the case. Also, after you have developed some experience negotiating Work-Out Plans, you will have the ability to quickly review the information on the Intake Form and determine how much work is involved so you can properly charge the Borrower(s).

Virtual Bankruptcy Assistants: If you are working for a bankruptcy attorney and the Borrower(s) have already filled out the Client Intake Forms for you to prepare their bankruptcy petition; you will already have this financial information. Therefore, you will not need to use these sample Intake Forms; the Client Intake Forms will be sufficient.

If you do not have a free copy of the Client Intake Forms that is used for bankruptcy clients, download them at: https://www.713training.com/intake_forms/

MY FORECLOSURE COMPANY
3333 Broad Boulevard, Suite 77
Lockbourne OH 43147
(740) 222-3333
http://www.myforeclosurecompany.com

Borrowers Name ⎯⎯⎯⎯⎯⎯⎯⎯⎯⎯⎯⎯
Social Security Number ⎯⎯⎯⎯⎯⎯⎯⎯⎯
Birthdate ⎯⎯⎯⎯⎯⎯⎯⎯⎯⎯⎯⎯⎯⎯⎯
Home Address ⎯⎯⎯⎯⎯⎯⎯⎯⎯⎯⎯⎯
City: ⎯⎯⎯⎯⎯⎯ State: ⎯⎯ Zip: ⎯⎯⎯⎯
Home Phone ⎯⎯⎯ Work ⎯⎯⎯⎯ Cell ⎯⎯⎯
Employer's Name ⎯⎯⎯⎯⎯⎯⎯⎯⎯⎯⎯
Title or Position ⎯⎯⎯⎯⎯⎯⎯⎯⎯⎯⎯

- continued on Page 100

- *continued from Page 99*

Employer's Address _____
City: _____ State: _____ Zip: _____
Employment Date _____
Annual Salary (from current paycheck stub)   _____
Gross Monthly Salary (before deductions)   _____
Monthly Earnings for Overtime Wages   _____
Monthly Earnings for Tips and Commissions   _____
Monthly Earnings for Bonuses   _____
Monthly Social Security Income   _____
Monthly Retirement Income   _____
Monthly Disability Income   _____
Monthly Income Received for Alimony   _____
Monthly Income Received for Child Support   _____
Total taxes deducted from
paycheck per month   _____
Total of other deductions per month   _____
What are these other deductions from your paycheck
for? _____

Co-Borrowers Name _____
Social Security Number _____
Birthdate _____
Home Address _____
City: _____ State: _____ Zip: _____
Home Phone _____ Work _____Cell _____
Employer's Name _____
Title or Position _____
Employer's Address _____
City: _____ State: _____ Zip: _____
Employment Date _____
Annual Salary (from current paycheck stub)   _____
Gross Monthly Salary (before deductions)   _____
Monthly Earnings for Overtime Wages   _____
Monthly Earnings for Tips and Commissions   _____
Monthly Earnings for Bonuses   _____

- *continued on Page 101*

- continued from Page 100

Monthly Social Security Income   _____
Monthly Retirement Income   _____
Monthly Disability Income   _____
Monthly Income Received for Alimony   _____
Monthly Income Received for Child Support   _____
Total taxes deducted from
paycheck per month   _____
Total of other deductions per month   _____
What are these other deductions from your paycheck
for? _____

Dependents

Name _____
Relationship _____
Date of Birth _____

Name _____
Relationship _____
Date of Birth _____

Name _____
Relationship _____
Date of Birth _____

Name _____
Relationship _____
Date of Birth _____

Property Information

Address: _____
City: _____ State: _____ Zip: _____

- continued on Page 102

- continued from Page 101

Is this property rented or does Borrower currently live in the house?
- ☐ Rented to tenant named:
- ☐ Borrowers currently live in the foreclosure property

Average Monthly mortgage payment _____
How many months are you behind in payments? _____
What is the total amount to catch up
all back payments? _____
What year did you first purchase the property? _____

Do you have a second or third mortgage on the property? ☐ YES ☐ NO
What type of loan do you have? ☐ FHA ☐ VA ☐ Conventional ☐ Other

How is the property held? ☐ individual ☐ trust ☐ community property ☐ corporate ☐ husband and wife as joint tenants ☐ husband and wife as community property ☐ Other

Financial Statement

Provide the current value of the assets you have for the following:

Cash on hand _____
Checking and savings accounts _____
Stocks, Bonds and Mutual Funds _____
401K or Other Retirement Account _____
Certificates of Deposit _____
Equity in current home _____
Other Real Estate _____

- continued on Page 103

- continued from Page 102

Automobiles or other Motor Vehicles

Year _____ Make _____ Model _____
Year _____ Make _____ Model _____
Year _____ Make _____ Model _____
Year _____ Make _____ Model _____

Other Assets

Life Insurance Cash Value   _____
Total of Any Other Assets   _____

Monthly Expenses

Provide the *average* monthly amount you pay for the
following expenses:

Monthly mortgage payment   _____
Average monthly payment for property taxes   _____
(if not included in mortgage payment)
Average monthly home insurance payment   _____
(if not included in mortgage payment)
Monthly Home owner association dues   _____
Rental payment (if you are not living   _____
in the home)
Average monthly utility costs   _____
Average monthly cost for telephones   _____
Average monthly cost for cable television   _____
Average monthly cost for internet service   _____
Average monthly cost for groceries   _____
Monthly child support paid to another person   _____
Monthly alimony paid to another person   _____
Average monthly child care expenses   _____
Average monthly elderly care expenses   _____

- continued on Page 104

- continued from Page 103

Average monthly medical expenses ———
(not covered by insurance) ———
Average monthly school tuition ———
Monthly payment for all car loans ———
Average monthly cost for car insurance ———
Average monthly cost for public transportation ———
Average monthly cost for credit card bills ———
Average monthly cost for clothing ———
Average monthly cost for college tuition ———
Other monthly expenses: ———

I (we) certify that the financial information provided on these Intake Forms, is true and correct to the best of my (our) knowledge and it is an accurate account of my (our) financial condition.

I (we) consent for **Mary Doe**, a Foreclosure Mediator, the mortgage Servicer, mortgage insurer and/or Freddie Mac, Fanny Mae, Ginnie Mae and the Veterans Administration to engage in discussions and negotiations with me (us) or my (our) designed representative regarding alternative programs to foreclosure. I (we) acknowledge that the above-referenced parties are under no obligation to agree to an alternative to foreclosure and that representation has not been made at any time by any party involved in this process, that my (our) mortgage will be modified or that an alternative to foreclosure will be authorized.

I (we) consent for **Mary Doe**, a Foreclosure Mediator, the mortgage Servicer, mortgage insurer and/or Freddie Mac, Fanny Mae, Ginnie Mae and the Veterans Administration to discuss and share information about

- continued on Page 105

- *continued from Page 104*

my (our) mortgage and personal financial situation with third parties such as purchasers, brokers, real estate agents, insurers, property inspections, financial institutions and/or creditors.

I (we) acknowledge that the payments on my (our) mortgage are delinquent and that any collection efforts currently in progress including foreclosure proceedings will continue without delay while relief from foreclosure options are being reviewed.

I (we) agree that discussions and negotiations of a possible workout alternative will not constitute a waiver of, or defense to, my (our) lender's right to commence or continue any foreclosure or other collection action. The foreclosure action will cease and an alternative to foreclosure will be provided only if, and when, my (our) lender has approved an agreement for a foreclosure alternative in writing and the agreed upon alternative is completed prior to foreclosure.

I (we) have had the opportunity to consult with legal and/or tax counsel prior to signing this document and I (we) willingly agree to these terms and conditions whether or not I (we) elect to retain such counsel.

_____

Borrower's Signature
Date _____

_____

Co-Borrower's Signature
Date _____

SECTION 4
Marketing and Business-Building Techniques for Foreclosure Mediators

Marketing a Foreclosure Mediation Service

At the beginning of this book I briefly touched on the different marketing approaches for virtual bankruptcy assistants and notary signing agents. Because virtual bankruptcy assistants are working with clients filing bankruptcy, they are already in touch with clients who are in foreclosure. Therefore, the work from the bankruptcy attorney, along with Foreclosure Mediation services is a winning combination for virtual bankruptcy assistants. In fact, virtual bankruptcy assistants may not even need to market their services. They will simply incorporate it as an additional service the attorney they are working for can provide to their clients.

However, if you are not working with an attorney, you can still locate people who are

need of your services. The following information provides you with several places to locate
your target market of customers:

♦ Property listings that are in foreclosure as well as upcoming Sheriff sales is public
information. Normally, these legal notices
published in your local legal newspaper. If they
are not, then call your local bar association and
ask them what publication the foreclosures and
Sheriff sales are listed. If the bar association
doesn't know, call the different newspapers in
you area until you find out where the foreclosures are published. Then subscribe to that
newspaper so you can keep updated on these
properties.

♦ Contact the Sheriff's office and find
out where you can obtain a list of future Sheriff
sales. The legal notices contain the property
address, value of the property, property

description and the name(s) of the Borrower(s). After obtaining this information, you can look up the Borrower's contact information online and contact them directly to introduce them to your Foreclosure Mediation services.

Some websites to help you locate people and addresses online are:

- http://www.infospace.com/
- http://www.peoplelookup.com/
- http://www.whitepages.com/
- http://find.intelius.com/
- http://www.zabasearch.com/
- http://www.zillow.com/
- http://www.peoplefinders.com/

You will find that you can do a free search on any of these websites but sometimes, the information you receive is limited. When I typed in my name at InfoSpace.Com it provided my street address as well as my telephone number. But when I typed in my next door neighbor's name, I did not get a telephone number. Instead, I was asked to pay a fee for more detailed information.

So, if you decide to provide Foreclosure Mediation services it would be to your benefit to join one of these services. Just visit all of them and choose the one you like to use the best. Then sign up for a membership.

As far as the price for these member-ships, all of them are different. For example, you can sign up and gain access to Intelius.Com's entire database without any upfront cost. You receive a username and password when you sign up and immediately you can begin using the system. However, when you request records, your credit card will be charged. At this time, the charge is $19.95

for a state-wide criminal records search and
$49.95 for a national criminal records search.

But PeopleFinders.Com currently charges
only $9.95 for a one-time report, $19.95 for a
24-hour membership (unlimited searches) or a
comprehensive background report for only
$39.99. I have used this service before and
they did an excellent job.

Of course you will not be able to afford to
pay $39.99 for every Borrower you find in the
foreclosure section of your local newspaper.
Therefore, the list of websites previously provided should provide you with enough contact
information to find most Borrower(s).

Potential Problems of Locating Borrower(s)

Even if you do find the address and telephone number of a Borrower to offer your

Foreclosure Mediation services to; there is a possibility they no longer live at the property. In fact, you will find that some people who are facing foreclosure will leave the property before the Sheriff serves the first foreclosure papers.

In this case, you will need to write a letter of introduction, mail it to the Borrower(s) address and hope they filed a Change of Address with their local post office. If they did, your letter will be forwarded to the new address. Or, if the forwarding order has expired, the post office will return the letter to you with the forwarding address so you can remail it.

Your letter of introduction should be something that gets right to the point. Also, the letter should be printed on your company letterhead and provide your web site address. The following is an example of the type of letter I am referring to.

Dear Captain James T. Kirk:

     I understand that your property at **123 Main Street, Lancaster, Ohio** is designated for a Sheriff's sale on **July 5, 2007.**

     If you are interested in saving your property as well as your equity (if any), I provide Foreclosure Mediation Services where I work with your Lender to negotiate a Work-Out Plan. Whether you are aware or not -- there may be many options available to you instead of foreclosure.

     FREE - NO CHARGE CONSULTATION.

     Please take a moment and call me right now at **777-111-2222.** I will ask you a few questions and let you know if my Foreclosure Mediation services can help you -- or visit my website at www.myforeclosurecompany.com. There you will find complete details as well as a free Borrower's Get-Started Package that you can download, print and fill out by hand. There is no cost or obligation.

     My job is to save your property and maintain your equity. I do not work for the Lender.
Instead, I work for YOU and for YOUR BENEFIT.
I look forward in speaking with you soon.

Sincerely,

Jack Sprat, Owner
My Foreclosure Company
http://www.myforeclosurecompany.com

Another Method of Finding Borrower(s) Who Need Your Services

A large majority of Borrower(s) who file bankruptcy are in foreclosure. Since bankruptcy filings are public information you can get the information online or through your local bankruptcy court.

For online court record searches visit:
http://pacer.psc.uscourts.gov/

Click on "Register" and you can get a free username and password. If you provide your credit card number, you gain immediate access to PACER's database after registration. The cost for accessing PACER's court records is currently only 8¢ per printed page; but your search is always free.

I strongly urge you to download and read the online PACER manual. It is available at:

http://pacer.psc.uscourts.gov/pacerdocs.html

Download the "Pacer Service Center User Manual" as well as the "Pacer and CM/ECF Brochure." Since you probably will be using PACER for numerous searches, instead of losing time trying to figure out the system on your own, it is much easier to take time now to read these documents. Believe me, they will save you a great deal of time and teach you how to make the most of your PACER searches.

Marketing Tip

When you start your Foreclosure Mediation business, do not be like most people and limit yourself to only contacting 5 or 10 Borrower(s). I have watched people do this in the past. I provide them with excellent resources and they contact a few people and then give up. Then, many of these people complain that they cannot make any money. Also (once in awhile), I even get blamed by people who think I was the reason they failed in business.

But the truth of the matter is that every topic I write a book about - I have personally experienced. I am not a writer who simply looks up information that was experienced by others and writes a book about it. I have actually lived, been a part of, or personally witnessed all the information I am providing to you in my books. If the information does not work for you, I cannot be blamed. But I can tell you that I have been successful with the business ideas I write about and I know 100s of other people who have been successful also. Therefore, your success is up to you. You are in control of your own destiny. Not me. All I can do is provide you with all the tools you need. It is up to you to pick up those tools and build your own empire.

Therefore, if you are going to contact Borrower(s) on your own, your success will only come from high numbers. Instead of contacting only 5 or 10 Borrower(s) who are facing foreclosure, contact at least 15 PER DAY. That's right. And if you run out of Borrower(s) in your area, get lists of Sheriff sales and people who filed bankruptcy in other areas. Remember, you have no limit to the people you can help with your services. You could live in Kit Carson, Colorado and perform Foreclosure Mediation services for someone in New York City. You will discover that many of the Lenders use the same Servicers; so it doesn't matter where you or where the Borrower(s) reside - which makes this the perfect virtual business.

Believe me; if you make it a point to contact at least 15 Borrower(s) every single day who are facing foreclosure, you will eventually get a Borrower who will use your service. You will discover that getting the first customer is the hard part for any new business. But once you do, the 2nd, 3rd and future customers will be easier to obtain. Then, after you have done a good job for your customers and they are happy with your service, they will tell others and you will get even more business.

Marketing Articles

The following section contains several articles that I have never published in any of my previous books. I hand selected them for publishing in "The Foreclosure Mediation Training Guide" because I believe they contain excellent and solid advice to help those of you starting and operating your own business.

Victoria Ring

ARTICLE 1
Are You Broke? Do You Need Money Right Now to Start Your Business?

Are You Broke? Do You Need Money Right Now to Start Your Business?

Often, our office receives telephone calls and emails from people who say something like this: *"How long will it take me to receive my order? I just quit my job and I need to make money next week."*

For those of you who have your own business, I am sure you chuckled at this question. But for those people just starting their first business, their minds are still focused on the "employee" mindset and they do not have a clue about how a business operates. If you fall into this category, this article is for you.

Then there are others who will buy training products, participate in all the seminars and training conferences, but they never do anything with the information. Instead, they are always seeking that "magic bullet" that will give them the confidence they need. Unfortunately, people waiting on others to supply their emotional needs will never be fulfilled. If you fall into this category, this article is for you.

First Things First

When you start a new business and you have very little money to invest into marketing and advertising, you cannot anticipate any business income for four to six months or even longer. The old saying *"You have to have money to make money."* is very true. However, you can make money if you start out with nothing. But the realization is: it will take much, much longer.

The Solution to the Problem

The solution to the problem is simple. If you have no money to start a business and you do not have a business partner with the money to invest, you must accept the fact that your business income is not going to pay your bills. You need to find another way to bring in enough personal income to pay your personal bills. Your business income should NEVER be used to pay your personal expenses. The business income your business earns is for the business; not your mortgage, food and electricity.

For example, my first year in business brought me an income of $1,700 and my expenses totaled $1,200. I certainly could not live on $500 a year. So what did I do? I moved out of my 2 bedroom apartment and into a basement efficiency to reduce my overhead expenses. Next, I got a job working for temporary agencies. The income from the temporary agencies paid my personal expenses and I was able to put all the income the business earned back into the business. When I did this, I slowly began to see an improvement in the success growth of my business.

Ideas for Finding Temporary Work

Back in 1988 the internet may have existed but the average person had never head of it. Therefore, I did not have the ability (like you do) to find employment through online methods. But fortunately, today, there are several choices available to you in finding immediate income to pay your personal expenses while you build your business. Let's examine a few of your options:

1. Sign up with legal temporary agencies which will put you in touch with attorneys. A few nationwide agencies are:

   http://www.affiliates.com
   http://www.lawjobs.com/
   http://www.lawdocsxpress.com/
   http://net-temps.com/jobs/temporary/index.htm

Note: You do NOT need to have a paralegal certificate to work in the legal field. You only need a paralegal certificate to work as a paralegal. There are many more positions in a law firm beside paralegals.

2. Work for real estate offices or law firms in your area. Even if you only have basic office skills you can answer the phone and take messages. This will put you in touch with attorneys who need your Foreclosure Mediation services.

Note: It is important for you to seek any job as long as it is in your chosen field of profession. This way, you have the ability to improve your skills and knowledge within the industry which will be worth its weight in gold as you are building your own business.

3. Think about getting your Real Estate license and learn the mortgage industry from

the inside out. If you are a good salesperson, you can earn an excellent income selling homes. Also, with a Real Estate license, you get access to privy information regarding foreclosures and Sheriff sales.

4. Think about working for creditor bankruptcy attorneys and learn the foreclosure process from the inside out. Creditor bankruptcy attorneys normally work out of large law firms so they normally have positions to fill.

To locate creditor bankruptcy attorney law firms, you can use the temporary agencies in your area or check with your local bar association for a list of creditor bankruptcy attorneys. You also can go online through PACER and look at bankruptcy petitions in your area. Check the debts on Schedule F until you find one that has been turned over to a law firm for collection. Get the name and address of the law firm, send a cover letter and resume and follow up within two weeks.

All of these ideas will help you to earn money while you are building your business. Why? Because if you are working within the industry you are starting a business in, you will become more successful faster. The reason being, you have more experience and knowledge than the average person. This places you at an advantage in building your business.

A Word of Caution

Let me end this article with one final word of caution: Do not approach a potential employer and say: *"I am starting my own business and I need to work for awhile to pay my bills. Do you have a job opening?"* This question will produce a "no" response.

Instead, you need to ask a "yes" question like: *"I am a Foreclosure Mediator who has receiving training in the foreclosure industry. I would like to advance my knowledge in creditor bankruptcy and I would love to work for your company. Do you have any jobs available for a hard working, dedicated employee?"*

The difference between the two approaches is that the second approach provides a value for the potential employer. The value is that you are interested in your work and will do a better job. The first approach provides no benefit to the employer; only you. Therefore, the first approach demonstrates a selfish and self-centered attitude which is a turnoff for employers. They probably have enough of those types of people already employed.

So get out your telephone book, classified ads and community papers. Start looking for

any job you can find in the foreclosure or mortgage industry. Continue working in the field
until your business is earning enough income to
pay the overhead expenses as well as a salary
to you that is larger than your present income.
At that point you can safely quit your job and all
of this will take time.

But even, if you are fortunate enough to
have some money saved back to pay your
personal expenses for awhile, it is still to your
benefit to first work in the field and gain some
experience. This step is imperative because
owning a business is not all fun and games. It
can be stressful and difficult at times. Without
a basic knowledge of the industry you are building a business in, you will not be able to face
the difficult times and your business has the
chance of being very short lived. When this
happens, you may never get back your determi-
nation to start a business again.

ARTICLE 2
How to Gain Knowledge
and Obtain Power
in Business

How to Gain Knowledge and Obtain Power in Business

Knowledge is not intelligence. Knowledge is something you obtain after repeatedly performing a skill or being trained in a skill. Knowledge has nothing to do with intelligence. You can have an IQ of 212 but you would never have the knowledge about everything there is to know.

But how do you obtain knowledge? Do you read books? Do you watch videos and attend seminars? Do you enroll in training courses? Do you communicate with people who have the knowledge you wish to obtain? The answer is YES to all four questions. But the problem is, many people don't know how to listen, read and communicate in order to obtain the knowledge provided to them.

The following are some tips to help you:

Listening Skills

1.   Pay close attention to the answer a person gives after you ask them a question. Although this sounds simple to do, the problem occurs when the listener does not listen. Instead, they are contemplating what they are going to say next, or even concentrating on unrelated matters. It takes a little effort to truly listen to what people are saying and putting all your own thoughts out of your mind for a moment so you can learn from them.

2.   Maintain eye contact with the speaker. This is a good exercise to get into a habit of doing because it will help you to become less distracted or keep your thoughts from wondering.

3.   Avoid the human tendency to jump to conclusions about what is said before the

speaker has finished. Instead, you should listen closely even if you think you know what the person is going to say. Think of yourself as a news reporter with unbiased views and gathering as much information as possible so you can write a detailed report later. Once you have fully understood and absorbed what the speaker is saying, you can form your own opinions at that time. But forming an opinion while the speaker is talking does not allow you to absorb knowledge.

4. Make sure you understand the entire concept before offering any advice or suggestions to others. Sometimes people are so eager to show their enthusiasm that they offer suggestions without realizing the speaker would prefer that they listen rather than give advice. This is not to say that suggestions and solutions are not important. Of course they are, if they are offered at the appropriate time.

5.   Stop everything you are doing and give the speaker your undivided attention. It is nearly impossible to concentrate on what someone is saying if you are doing something else. You may be able to take in the gist of what it being said, but you will never absorb all the details. Details are the meat and potatoes of knowledge and should never be missed.

Reading Skills

1.   When you read a paragraph make sure you can repeat the meaning of that paragraph before you read any further. It is natural for your mind to wander as you are reading a training manual or other reading material. But you need to train yourself to read and understand every paragraph before you move on to the next. This does not mean that you will gain all the knowledge from that paragraph – just that you understand what the writer is saying.

2. Read with an open, unbiased mind until you fully understand what the writer is conveying. You are trying to obtain knowledge that you currently do not have. If you allow your own biased opinions to clutter up your mind while you are trying to obtain that knowledge, you will get little benefit from the knowledge the writer is giving to you.

3. Always read a book with a yellow highlight marker in your hand. Use it to highlight sentences, paragraphs and sections that stick out as important to you. This way, you can go back through the book and immediately find all the highlighted areas during your second review.

Telephone Skills

1. Organize your thoughts before making the call. No one appreciates a telephone call

from a person who takes forever to get to the point. Garbled requests for information can only have one result – failure. You need to organize your thoughts before making the telephone call so you can get right to the point and resolve the issue. If necessary, write down a list of the questions you need to ask or what information you need to obtain; then refer to it when you make the telephone call.

2.   Do not put a caller on hold for longer than 1 minute. If you discover you cannot answer the question or solve the problem during the time the caller is on hold, offer to call them back as soon as you have an answer. Then remember to call them back. Most people will wait for you to call them back if you promised to do so. If you still are unable to get the information to help them within 1 hour after promising to call them back, call them anyway and explain that it will take longer than expected.

Then, give the caller an expected wait time for you to get the information or solve the problem.

3.   Take notes during the telephone call. When someone calls you, train yourself to write down the name of the person and any other notes pertinent to the conversation. This way, you can refer to the person by name during the rest of the conversation and record important information you will use when you hang up the phone.

4.   End the telephone call appropriately. Normally the person who calls should be the one who ends the call. But if the caller continues to talk forever and you need the call to end, be professional. Wait for a pause and say something like: *"I am sorry to interrupt but I have another appointment. Perhaps we can talk later but thank you again for calling."*

5.   Return all your calls promptly. A hectic and demanding schedule is no excuse for failing to return a telephone call. Have you ever tried to reach someone repeatedly by telephone, only to have them call you back several days later and tell you they had been so busy they could not call you back? If so, you can imagine how a customer or client will feel when you do the same to them.

Business Email Communications

1.   Use the subject line of an email message to inform. The importance of an email is often determined by the subject line. Keep the subject line brief and specific. Make sure it relates to the subject matter of your email. If not, the receiver might accidentally delete it or mistake your email as spam or an unsolicited advertisement.

2. Treat emails like business letters. It is better to be more formal than casual in business email communications. You want to make a good impression.

3. Include a signature line. Nothing is more annoying than receiving an email from someone you want to contact but they provide no name, title, company, telephone number or website information. Do not rely on people being able to reply to your email as their only means to contact you. Often, email can bounce (due to internet glitches) through no fault of your own and your email is never received.

4. Never shout at people by using uppercase letters. Typing in uppercase letters is considered CYBER SHOUTING. As an alternative use asterisks to emphasize words, such as: Please contact us "no later" than Friday.

5.   Skip the fancy decorations. Vivid colors, flashing symbols of bouncing smiley faces (better known as emotions) should never be used in business communications. These types of effects should only be reserved for personal email, not business email.

6.   Keep your email very brief. Writing long emails about how you emotionally feel about a situation does not get your email read. But do not be too brief either. Provide the business with all the pertinent facts so they have enough information to look up your records and resolve the issue the first time. However, if your email is longer than 2 paragraphs, pick up the phone and call the company to resolve the issue.

7.   Remember that no email is private. Every email you send passes through 1,000s of servers before it is delivered to the recipient. Additionally, every email you send is likely to be

achieved on 1,000s of computers who make it a point to back up their customer's email data. If you are angry and exhibit irrational behavior in an email, chances are it will come back to haunt you one day.

8.   Avoid mood mail. Email messages that convey strong emotions can be easily misunderstood. Never send an email when you are angry. Take time to cool down, count to 100, then go back and re-read your email and edit it before clicking the Send button.

9.   Proof every email before sending it to a business. It pays to check your grammar, spelling and punctuation before clicking the Send button. Getting in a hurry does nothing but cost you more time in the long run.

10.   Respect the privacy of others. When you send an email that you also want sent to

other people, use the BCC (blind carbon copy) function instead of the CC (carbon copy) function. This way, when the person receives your email, there will not be a long list of other email addresses at the top; and they don't have to scroll down through the list to get to the email message.

11. Be very cautious when you use the "Reply All" button on your email program. If you receive an email that was sent to a multitude of people, hitting the "Reply All" button will send your reply to everyone. Unless you want this to happen, do not use this feature.

12. Do not be a pest. If you do not receive a response within 24 hours after sending an email, either send a different email explaining why you are following up or pick up the phone and call the company.

13. Never send an attachment unless you have permission to do so. Most email servers today will automatically strip attachments because they can be considered spam. Unless the company has specifically requested that you send an attachment, never send one.

14. Think twice before sending jokes, chain letters or funny messages. Just because you may think something is funny or cute does not mean the person receiving it will feel the same way. In fact, they may even find them insulting. Do not risk your reputation.

15. When posting a response to a message board, remember that your email is forever edged in stone. Many people forget that when they post a message to a message board, that message is archived forever. The main website that archives every web site that has ever been in existence is The Wayback Machine at:

http://web.archive.org/

Article Summary

I sincerely hope that you have read this entire article and will use it to improve your communication and listening skills. When you do, you will find that your knowledge will increase and you will become a better asset for the attorneys and business associates you communicate with on a daily basis.

ARTICLE 3
The Importance of Really Listening to the Successful and Experienced for Free Advice

The Importance of Really Listening to the Successful and Experienced for Free Advice

At a meeting the other day I met a lady who asked if she could talk to me about her business and pick my brain for some marketing ideas. I said *"Sure. I would love to help you if I can."* Over lunch she proceeded to tell me all about her wonderful company in which she sold informational products concerning credit repair services.

Next, she said the problem she was having was that no one would attend the free meetings she offered that would introduce people to this wonderful service. I continued to question her and it appeared she had been taught some excellent marketing techniques, (probably knowledge that came from a money-making course she paid a fee to join) but she lacked the knowledge of understanding her customers.

One thing she could not understand is why everyone was not as excited about this service as she was. The answer was simple: People didn't know everything about the service like the lady talking to me had. Instead of being mad at people and complaining about how stupid people were for turning down this opportunity - she should have been telling people about her personal experiences using the service, or at least the experiences of others.

I also discovered that my initial suspicion was right. The marketing techniques she was using were the marketing techniques taught to her by the people at the marketing seminar she attended. In fact, this lady also purchased $250 of extra tapes and books that guaranteed she would succeed. Unfortunately, after doing everything she was trained to do – she was making very little money. I then waited for her to ask me for suggestions to help her. She never did. Therefore, I took the initiative to try and offer my thoughts, so I said: *"First of all. It doesn't matter what product or service you are trying to sell, if you are not making any money – you are doing something wrong in your marketing. Period. Since what you are doing is not working, let's look at some OTHER ways to market your business."*

To my surprise – this lady immediately changed the subject. She did not want a solution. She had been programmed by these "so-called" marketing gurus and was unable to listen to any other possible solutions.

However, if I could have, I would have told her that her product was destine for failure from the start. Why? Because any company that charges you money to learn how to become wealthy is nothing but trash. Companies like this make their money from the sale of their videos and books – not from the sale of their products. Legitimate companies like Mary Kay, Avon, Shaklee, etc. make the major part of their money from the sale of their products, which is why their products are well worth the price. Also, you will notice that Mary Kay, Avon and Shaklee never make claims that you will become wealthy overnight, drive new cars, move into a mansion and take cruises to the Caribbean whenever you feel like it. My dear – these are pipe dreams.

Secondly, this lady needed to target her market to people who were having credit problems. Whatever you are led to believe, not everyone in the world has credit problems. I know hundreds of people who have good or excellent credit and they would never be interested in attending a seminar for repairing their credit. If I could have talked to her further, I would have tried to help her pinpoint her target market – but unfortunately, she passed up an opportunity to help herself and turned me away. What a shame.

Oh well .. by publishing this article in my newsletter perhaps it will help you to open your eyes and LISTEN to others who know more than you do. Seek out people more educated and successful than yourself and learn what they do to become successful. And stop wasting your time with pipe dream promises.

ARTICLE 4
The Proper Way to
As for Help from
Successful People

The Proper Way to Ask for Help from Successful People

For those of you who have experienced parenthood you will be able to understand the following scenario.

Suppose you received an email one day that said: *"Could you tell me everything about raising a child from infancy through adulthood?"*

Would you be able to sufficiently answer this question in an email? Even if you called the person who sent you the email, how many weeks and months would it take you to cover your personal experience in raising a child from infancy to adulthood? And even if you spent the time detailing all your experiences, you still would never be able to cover every possible scenario because every child is different and every parent if different.

This is exactly the same thing I face when someone sends me an email that says: *"Can you tell me how to market my business?"*

I am faced with trying to figure out how in the world I could possibly answer this question. First of all, there are millions of ways to market a business just like there are millions of ways of raising a child. I can only tell you what worked for me. It is up to you to obtain input from MANY successful people so you can pick and choose the best marketing methods for you and your business.

All I can tell people who email me such open-ended questions is that it would take months to answer their question. I then suggest they read everything on the website, order a book and then email me with any specific questions. (I love helping people but only those who want to help themselves.)

So for those of you who have worked for an employer your entire life, it would be impossible for you to immediately know how to market a business. In the past, you relied on your employer to bring work into the company to keep you busy. If this describes your marketing knowledge, the first step is to read and study from a variety of successful people. Then read and study some more. Do your own research and educate yourself. But never email a person and ask them to provide you with every known marketing secret in the world. That approach shows that you are a beginner and many people won't even reply to your email.

ARTICLE 5
How Unprofessional Methods
Hurt Your Business Growth

How Unprofessional Methods Hurt Your Business Growth

This past week I received about 25 email messages that all said something similar to this:

"I am unemployed at this time but would like to know if I can get a "deep" discount on your bankruptcy and notary book. If you don't want to, I will understand."

My first thought was: *"Do people who write email messages like this go to the store and ask them to deeply discount a computer desk because they are unemployed and want to start a business?"* I don't think so. The average person will pay the price for the items they wish to purchase and if they don't have the money they won't buy them. But for some reason, a few people believe that by offering an "excuse" another person will feel sorry for them and give away free merchandise out of the goodness of their heart.

Wake up folks! This is NOT how you start out marketing a business and building a professional image for yourself in the industry! You should NEVER send out business communications that depict your company as poor and struggling.

Back when I started my first business I had a budget of $10 per week for advertising. I would have loved to have had the money to buy an advertisement in Small Business Opportunities magazine, but their ad rates were $150. It never entered my mind to write a letter to Small Business Opportunities magazine and tell them I was a poor, struggling company and request they discount their advertising to give me a chance. That would be like "begging" and I took a great deal of pride in my business. I made sure that every company I communicated with thought of me as a solid company that was rapidly expanding. This is the key to doing business with other businesses. No successful business owner wants to work with a poor and struggling company. But they will work with a company who is on a limited budget who offers something in return for their time and help.

Secondly, people who send out emails telling others they are poor (just to get something free or low cost) has no idea how bad this looks to the other person. But think about it - if some-one cannot afford to purchase the information they need to start their business, how in the world do they expect to build a business? This is the first sign that this person is not "on the ball" and probably not very serious.

A business needs money to survive and prosper. Just like you cannot survive without money, your business cannot survive without money either. If you believe you can start a business with absolutely no money, you are mistaken. An up-front investment must be made in order to obtain the materials you need to start your business. If you cannot afford them – work and save up the money until you can. Don't make your business look small and worthless by sending out communications claiming your business is poor and struggling. No serious business person will respond to that type of message.

Thirdly, the 25 or so people who emailed me their request to discount my products NEVER once offered me a price. They used words like "discount" and "price break". I wish just one person would have said *"I am offering you $40.00,"* but not one of them quoted any specific price. They wanted to leave it up to me to do the work for them – which was another mistake when you are negotiating prices with companies. A proper communication would be something like this:

> Ms. Ring:
>
> I have read your books and thoroughly enjoyed them. *(Always start a business email with a compliment.)* I would like to know if you offer discounts on your products or if you are anticipating any future coupon specials where I may purchase additional products at a reduced price? At this time, my company is on a limited budget but I would eventually like to purchase all your products. Thank you for your time and consideration.

Now this is the way to write a business email when you are seeking to save money. Do you see the differenc between the letter above and an email saying: *"Can you give me free books because I am poor and cannot afford it."*

Additionally, to end the email with a sentence like *"If you don't want to I will under-*

stand" is a ridiculous statement. Of course I don't want to. What would make these people think I woke up this morning looking for ways to giveaway my products so my company does not make any money? What's in it for me?

The serious business person would have waited until they had the money and ordered the products they wanted. Or, they would have made an offer to provide me with a benefit for giving them the discount.

In summary, do not make the mistake of letting other companies know you are a poor and struggling company. Never use this as an attempt to make them feel sorry for you. Instead, act like a resonsible business person who has pride in their business. As the old saying goes: Never let them see you sweat.

WEBSITE REFERENCES

WebSite References

Although the focus of this book has been on training you to help the Borrower negotiate a Work-Out Plan, this is only one small area of the foreclosure industry. Another area is where people buy foreclosed properties and resell them for a profit. Some people who do this for a living are legitimate and honest -- but a large majority are fraudulent. However, there is one company that claims to provide training in buying foreclosed property. Their website is at: http://www.foreclosureuniversity.com/

Foreclosure State Laws

http://2-stop-foreclosure.com/states/state.htm

Online Foreclosure Mediation Companies

http://www.foreclosureassistance.com/aboutus.html
http://foreclosuremediation.net/
http://earthangelsunited.org/9.html

http://www.walkawayplan.com/

http://www.reinstate.com/

Software for Judgment Recovery

http://www.wizlegal.com/

Bankruptcy Asset Sales

http://www.realtytrac.com/

Bankruptcy Leads and Marketing Services

http://www.bankruptcydb.com/

Foreclosure Listings

http://www.foreclosures.com/

http://www.foreclosure.com/

http://www.foreclosurefreesearch.com/

http://www.hud.gov/homes/homesforsale.cfm

http://chicago.dailyherald.il-foreclosure.com/

A Sample of Other Training Products Developed by 713TRAINING.COM

for a list of all products visit
http://www.713training.com/shop

The Foreclosure Mediation Training Package
Contains almost 5 hours of recorded information with three expert foreclosure mediators. Each provide insider knowledge and information about the field to help you grow and prosper your business. Also includes all the handouts from the teleconferences. Audios are in WAV and MP3 formats.

How to Start a Virtual Bankruptcy Assistant Service
ISBN: 0976159171, 348 pgs
The information contained in **How to Start a Virtual Bankruptcy Assistant Service** is a great tool to increase the skills of paralegals and other legal staff employed at bankruptcy law firms. It also is currently the ONLY training source available for virtual bankruptcy assistants. In addition, attorneys have used the training material in this book to set up their own bankruptcy practice. This information is NOT taught in any law school or paralegal training course.

The Virtual Bankruptcy Assistant Training Workbook
ISBN: 097615918X, 248 Pages
This workbook contains a complete set of Client Intake Forms as well as the final draft of the bankruptcy petition. Use it to prepare your practice petition from the information on the Client Intake Forms; then print out your document. Compare your document with the actual Chapter 7 bankruptcy petition and immediately recognize your mistakes so you can learn where your weak areas are. This is an extremely fast and easy way to advance your virtual bankruptcy assistant skills. The workbook also contains additional tips and techniques and several quizzes to test your knowledge.

Complete Video Training Package
Length: Over 9 hours

These 10 videos are digitally pro-duced directly on the computer screen. Narrated by Victoria Ring, she walks you through every line of the bankruptcy petition. You can follow along with every mouse movement and accelerate your learning curve in developing your skill in drafting bankruptcy petitions. This skill is now in great demand due to the recent changes in the bankruptcy law. In fact, many attorneys are still finding it difficult to keep up with all the form changes. But when you learn this skill, you will never be out of work because law firms need people skilled in drafting bankruptcy petitions in order for their law practice to thrive.

To order any of these products or for more information, visit:

http://www.713training.com/shop/cart.php

New products are developed frequently by Victoria Ring. Also, remember to subscribe to the free newsletter so you can be kept up-to-date with important updates and insider news. To subscribe, type in your name address and name at

http://www.713training.com

Attention Attorneys

A special website has been designed specifically for attorneys working in debtor bankruptcy and foreclosure. Visit the website below:

http://www.bankruptcyattorneytraining.com

Prayer for Your Success

I would like to thank you for purchasing this book. Because I give the credit and praise to Jesus Christ for my success in life, I will end this book with a prayer for your success:

Dear Lord: I ask that the information in this book be used to benefit the lives of others who are interested in the field of Foreclosure Mediation. I pray that you open their minds and bless them to succeed and grow strong, respectable businesses that will glorify your name and purpose. I ask this in Jesus's name ... Amen.

Graphico Publishing
http://www.graphicopublishing.com